:Spilling the Beans on...

Boudicca

tale of love and romans

First published in 2000 by Miles Kelly Publishing,
Bardfield Centre, Great Bardfield, Essex CM7 4SL

Printed in Italy

ISBN 1-902947-61-4

24681097531

Cover design and illustration: Inc
Layout design: GardnerQuainton

To Sue, Rebecca, Toby, JoJo and Dennis
– thanks to you all! – David R. Morgan

Spilling the Beans on...

Boudicca

a tale of love and romans

by David R. Morgan

Illustrations   Mike Mosedale

About the Author

David R. Morgan teaches 11–19 year-olds at Cardinal Newman School in Luton, and lives in Bedfordshire with his wife and two children.

David has been an arts worker and literature officer, organizer of book festivals and writer-in-residence for education authorities, a prison and a psychiatric hospital (which was the subject of a Channel 4 film, *Out of Our Minds*).

His books for children include: *The Strange Case of William Whipper-Snapper*, three *Info Rider* books for Collins and *Blooming Cats* which won the Acorn Award and was recently animated for BBC2's *Words and Pictures Plus*. David has also written poetry books, including: *The Broken Picture Book*, *The Windmill and the Grains* (Hawthorn Prize) and *Buzz Off*.

CONTENTS

CHAPTER 1

BABY BOU
how do you do?

Boudicca was born in AD 20 at the time of Beltane.

You what?
Beltane. Ancient Briton for 21st March. The Britons' priests were called druids. They loved this date because this was when their gods of nature were at their most powerful.

POW! They often celebrated by chopping off a head or two.

Boudicca was a royal Celt and proud of it. Celts had been top people in Britain for 1000 years before the birth of Christ. When they came, so did the Iron Age.

Tell us more about them, then.
They lived in forts with huge earth walls. Maiden Castle in the south of England is one of them. They also dwelt in farms, towers (called *broches*) and lake dwellings. These were all built as defences against warriors from different tribes, who liked nothing better than kissing their horses and painting their chariots before going out on raids or

whipping up a bit of war. Yes, all Celts loved a good fight, and if there was no-one else around they'd just fight each other.

'MEET THE ANCESTORS' SPECIAL

Boudicca was in the Iceni tribe. You want to know where the Iceni came from? Well, these Celtic warlords travelled to Britain from Germany in 1000 BC. They took over completely and were VERY HAPPY, THANK YOU with their new country. Soon you could see their hill forts watching over the landscape everywhere you went.

"SUITS YOU SIR, SUITS YOU"
Their fashion came from back in the trendy Celtic heartlands – southern Germany. They knew how to make iron, and soon their abstract art was much sought after. Quite a few masterpieces in it, too. They were also very successful farmers, living in their round houses. By the time the Romans came the Celts had achieved a real British civilization that they were very proud of. And why shouldn't they be? The rest of the world wasn't the great bunch of savages the Romans thought it was.

Next week: Priest kings and your own cut-out-and-build Stonehenge. If you're lucky.

What about Boudicca?

Ah yes. Boudicca had red hair and big flashing eyes and was definitely full of this warrior blood. But when she was young she was artistic. She loved making gold pins.

What for?

The Iceni tribe that Boudicca belonged to was very rich. Her father, Bontenicca, really liked seeing his little girl enjoying herself. If gold pins pleased her, then gold pins it would be. The Iceni lived in what we now call Norfolk, though their lands stretched into Suffolk and Cambridgeshire.

What about her early life?

Her mother died giving birth to her. A druid, Monatacus, looked after her. He carved wooden dolls and she really loved them. But...

But what?

She took them to the sacred oak groves and MADE THEM FIGHT EACH OTHER. Think of it: "Take that!" "No, you take that, you nostril gleam!" The dolls often ended up in bits. So Monatacus just carved a few more. Ah, Boudicca was a true Celt.

You mean she broke all her toys?

That as well. But mainly she was brave and that's what Celts were known for – bravery in battle. "You looking at me? YOU

LOOKING AT *ME*?" Not a good thing to do with a Celt around, especially as they fought with nothing on at all except a blue dye called woad painted on from head to foot.

And they didn't just fight for fun. Bravery in battle gave them the BIGGEST MERIT MARK OF ALL and secured them a place in the afterlife. Well worth waiting for. What does an arm or leg sliced off matter if you've got *that*?

So her gold pins wouldn't do her much good, then?
Not at all. These Celts might have been warlike, but they also liked pretty things. They made bronze mirrors, enamelled

jewellery, rich weapons, household goods of all kinds. They didn't read or write: their skills were passed from one generation to the next by word of mouth. Boudicca wore a short-sleeved tunic reaching down to her ankles and often displayed jewellery that set off her magnificent red hair.

I'm getting the picture about her.

Good. Warlike and artistic. Both together. That was Boudicca. She belonged to the warrior aristocracy as neatly as a sword fits its sheath. What a life! – raids on other tribes, farming and then gut-busting feasts in the great hall. Huge chunks of meat were devoured. Pork was the favourite. Gallons of wine and beer followed them down.

Think about them there. The men wore long moustaches which trapped food while they ate. Their drink was strained through both moustache and food, giving it a fatty flavour.

On second thoughts, don't think about them.

Everybody sat on the floor on animal skins. They stuffed their faces until they grew tired and then simply rolled over and fell asleep. Many was the time that Boudicca would wake up with a sizeable piece of pig stuck between her teeth.

What then, after she woke up?
She would grab a lump of herb-scented animal fat and go for a soak in the nearby stream. Then she would watch Radicca, an old woman who was like a second mother to her, make brooches, bracelets, necklets of twisted metal called torques – and soup from pigs' brains and grass.

Don't think about that either!

Is that all she did in her life?
Oh no. Destiny was calling. Boudicca grew up. Everyone respected her. She could wrestle a horse – and talk its hind leg off as well.

Yet sometimes, as darkness came, Boudicca would sit silent in the moonlit, starlit oak groves and listen to ancient, wind-whispering voices which stirred her blood and heart. Sometimes she was watched. Prasutagus, young and cautious, had followed her. He made up his mind that this strong-willed, beautiful girl would be his. It was his dream.

Sometimes dreams do come true.

Did this one?

Yes. The more Prasutagus followed her with gifts of enamel and twirly love designs that he drew for her, sitting on animal skins during long Celtic evenings full of ghosts, magic and imaginings, the more Boudicca grew to love him. They shared a lot. Celts had been there so long that the land was their lives. That was what the druids celebrated. Woe betide anyone who tried to take it away.

So did they get married?

Indeed they did. Everyone celebrated the wedding of fiery Boudicca and practical Prasutagus. Both were of royal birth. Antedios, High King of the Iceni, was there and the druid Monatacus bound the young couple together. Even the leaves on the ancient, sacred oaks seemed to clap as wind wound through them. Yes, it was quite an event.

14

How did they get on?

Very well. Prasutagus loved watching his wife as she walked and talked. She was so tall, with flashing eyes and red hair flowing down to her knees. Her multi-coloured tartan tunic touched her ankles and she held her warlike spear of authority.

"Oh, how I love you, Bou," he would say. From this love came two daughters. But no son.

"No problem," said Prasutagus. "We are strong. Nothing can harm us."

And Boudicca almost smiled.

What's in a name? Boudicca or Boadicea?

Most certainly Boudicca. Well, most probably! We don't know her exact name, but whatever it was, the Romans latinized it as Boudicca. 'Boadicea' only came many centuries after her death. People thought it sounded more feminine and romantic.

Boudicca would probably have hated it!

* * * *

CHAPTER 2

ROAMING ROMANS

Do you remember what the Celts felt about their land?

Of course. It was their lives. Woe betide anyone who tried to take it away.

Dead right. So what might have happened next?

Did someone try to take it away?

Not just try. They DID. The Romans. The Emperor Claudius might have a terrible stutter, but he sure knew what he wanted to complete his great empire.

B-B-B-BRITAIN.

A few Romans lived here already. Julius Caesar had brought an army 100 years before. He didn't stay, but left a few of his countrymen to keep an eye on things.

But now, in AD 43, came the real thing: the BIG TAKEOVER.

They swept in and set up a capital at Camulodunum (Colchester to you). But soon their money and trade capital, which grew quickly, was at Londinium (better known now, perhaps, as LONDON). Londinium. Great place for a neat night out – if you liked bear baiting. Nearly as good as the Millennium Dome. No Christians to throw to lions yet, though. Sorry.

So what did the Celts do about that?
What could they do? Wise Antedios, High King of the Iceni, became friends with the Romans and signed a peace with them. That way he protected his tribe, territory and wealth. But age can be a high price to pay for wisdom and, being very old, Antedios died in AD 49.

Then what?

Things became unstable. The Romans thought they'd better confiscate some of the Iceni weaponry.

But the Iceni didn't like this one bit and they fought back. This was beginning to turn rather nasty. However – who should become king but:

PRASUTAGUS,

Who, Boudicca's husband?

The same. And he calmed things down. He made a deal with the emperor.

"Look, let's be friends. When I die my Iceni lands can be divided 50/50 between you and my daughters. Not bad, eh?"

"Not bad? Pah!"

Who said that?

Who do you think? Was it:

a) the Emperor Claudius?

b) the king's priest, Monatacus?

c) the king's people, the rest of the Iceni?

All of them, I suppose?
You're probably right. Nobody really likes a compromise. But the one who said it loudest was:

d) the king's wife, Boudicca.

Oh, dear.

Boudicca didn't trust the Romans as far as she could throw a pig. Still, she kept quiet and the deal was made. For a time, Iceni and Romans lived fairly peaceably.

The Romans treated Prasutagus as King of the Britons – but only in name. They made a good deal out of business, trade and land. Prasutagus smiled and saw his family grow up safely. The Romans rubbed their hands and counted the cash.

Boudicca's daughters liked watching the Celtic men bleach their hair. They washed it in lime until the roots were blond and the ends stiff and spiky. The daughters liked to stick berries on the longest spikes.

Fruity or what? These girls were definitely growing up.

Why was Boudicca so angry? This all sounds rather nice.
Just wait. The Romans didn't like druids. They thought these
priests were their worst enemies. And they were. They were
the ones who stirred up all the hatred of the Romans and
urged the Britons to fight . The druids would have to be got rid
of. So, between AD 47 and AD 60 , that's what the Romans did,
until only 'Mona', the druid stronghold in Wales, remained.

Frumentum News
(update)

HUMAN SACRIFICE: EMPEROR SPEAKS OUT

The row between the emperor and the druids took a turn for the worse today. The Chief Druid and his priests have been invoking the magical powers of their gods in ceremonies in waterside groves all over Britain. "STOP DOING THIS," the emperor commands.

A sandstone pillar of a three-headed god is used in the ceremony. Beside it stands a cauldron holding blood, buckets and buckets of blood, from human and animal sacrifices.

"Don't do this. Blood… schmud! Dump the stuff and don't do it again," says the emperor.

The Druids hang ritual objects from trees in sacred oak groves and throw sacred body parts into the water.

"Stop all this stuff now… or else!" says the emperor.

"Or else what?" say the druids.

"YOU'LL SEE," the emperor answers.

One final push was needed to get rid of the druids for ever. Most of the Roman army from Camulodunum, Londinium and Verulamium (St Albans) was in Wales. Their leader was Caius Suetonius Paulinus. In AD 60 he had the army that was to bring the druids to their destruction.

Meanwile, back at home – disaster!

Tell us, tell us!

In AD 60 , Prasutagus was hunting in the great forest. A wild pig startled his horse. Prasutagus was thrown against the branch of an ancient oak. The oak branch went through his stomach. Two days later he was dead.

Boudicca wept and the whole tribe wailed. Things would never be the same again.

Poor Boudicca.
I know. She loved Prasutagus and respected the way he tried to keep the kingdom together. She remembered the moonlit oak groves, his twirly love designs and all the good times.

But time waits for no man and has no feelings.

Boudicca had always kept her bad feelings about the Romans to herself. After all, her daughters were lively and happy teenagers. She watched them sing and dance and do those unusual things with berries. Monatacus looked on. "It's not so bad," he said. "Though I'm a druid, the Romans don't know I'm here. Perhaps they'll leave us alone. If we give them half our lands, they'll be satisfied."

Boudicca wasn't so sure. She had watched Romans growing fat on the land of Britain and didn't think the 50/50 idea was a goer. "Bad is never good until worse happens."

She prayed to her gods that night. The ageless stars sparkled strangely and in a waking dream she saw the rivers of Britain turn to blood.

*   *   *   *

CHAPTER 3

AN EYE FOR AN ICENI

The Emperor Claudius was dead. Nero was emperor now. Gaius Decianus was Head Roman in Britain and he knew Nero was always on the fiddle and wanted everything the Iceni owned. The deal with Prasutagus meant nothing. So Gaius sent officers from Londinium to see what the Iceni land was worth and bring back half the jewels and livestock, especially the beautiful horses that the Iceni treasured. But the officers took a lot more than half.

Did Boudicca let them?

She did her best not to. "This is bad," she said to her daughters. "I can't let them get away with it."

The Roman officers burst like brutes into her village and started to take whatever they wanted. But Boudicca stood in their way.

"Stop!" she commanded. "I am a queen and you will show me respect. Honour my husband's deal with you."

Two grabbed her. She knocked one out with a stone and threw the other on to a fire, giving him a very hot seat indeed.

But the Romans thought she was just a savage. They overcame her and then stripped and whipped her. They beat up and abused her daughters and cut the throat of the druid Monatacus. Then, laughing out loud, they left, taking everything they could.

Ah, everything's funny so long as it happens to someone else. They thought that Boudicca and the Iceni were *nothing*.

BIG MISTAKE!

So what did she do about it:
a) Nothing but sit at home and sulk?

b) Go to Gaius, complain about the soldiers and ask for everything back?

c) Rise up in rebellion, even though the Roman army was the greatest the world had ever seen?

Well, she couldn't do **a)**. It wasn't in her nature.

She wouldn't do **b)**. Prasutagus had tried reasoning with Romans and look where it had got them all.

No. It would have to be **c)**. After all, the Romans were just laughing at the Iceni. They were treating them like

28

slaves and taking whatever they wanted. Boudicca wasn't having this. She rose up and set her flashing eyes on their destruction.

"Lambs to the slaughter will be on every Roman tomb. Our Celtic forefathers will guide us as we crush this foe and reclaim our sacred land."

Boudicca never slept, anyway. She gathered all the Iceni together and then got their neighbours, the Trinovantes, to join them. The Trinovantes truly *hated* the Romans. All listened as she spoke, waving her spear polished murder-bright.

"Roman hearts are brittle as clay bowls. Our hearts are of ancient firm oak. Let our Celtic strength burst out over the whole of the great earth shield and kick Roman backsides from here to dung-filled Rome. Better still, let's KILL 'EM ALL."

Boudicca gathered more and more Britons outraged by Roman behaviour and ready to rebel.

The Romans would stop laughing as soon as the heads began to roll. Boudicca, her daughters by her side, was a master at stirring up Celtic blood. From all over East Anglia, British warriors walked behind Queen Boudicca's wickerwork chariot, with the courage of those with nothing to lose.

But they'd get hammered, surely.
Well, in the end an eye for an eye leads to blindness, but now

the Britons couldn't see that. The Romans had treated them like stupid children, told to shut up, sit quietly and do as they were told, while the Romans did what they liked. "Listen to teacher, children, and let us take everything you love. If you misbehave, you can't dream what will happen."

But nobody can go on talking like that to people all the time. The burning fury of Boudicca's rebels would be beyond anything the Romans could ever have dreamed of.

CHAPTER 4

THE CLOBBERING OF
CAMULODUNUM

So there was a real big battle, was there?
No, not really. Yes, Camulodunum in Essex was a busy place all
right. But there were only 200 Roman soldiers in it.

Even the temple to Claudius wasn't finished yet. The workers
were on strike over how much bread they got each day and
because the wine breaks weren't long enough. However,
finished or not, the temple was a symbol of Roman rule. The

Iceni hated it. They hated the "oh so clever, arty-farty statues" round it as well.

Where was the Roman army, then?
I told you. Still out in Wales, led by Paulinus and hammering druids. Paulinus had no idea about Boudicca and the 30,000 men following her. The warriors were so enthusiastic – "Here we go, here we go, here we go!" – if rather disorganized. They were armed with spears, swords, slings or just sharp sticks. The upper classes rode in wicker chariots.

They knew they would win. Soothsayers had told them so. When the tide went out on the coast, the sands were shaped like dead bodies and there was a horrible smell in the nearby forests for days. So they were bound to, weren't they?

I suppose so. Who could argue with that smell?
Anyway, Boudicca's army poured out of Norfolk and headed south.

"Your hearts are free. Have the courage to follow them," she shouted.

Only 200 Roman soldiers could be spared from Londinium. Even so, all the British living in Camulodunum were just like Romans themselves now. They heard about these approaching hordes. But they didn't worry about them. They persuaded the Roman settlers that Boudicca was miles away and would never dare attack.

"Look, no problem. Bou and her little band are lost in the forests. We're strong. Rome's might is behind us. If ever they get here, we'll be ready. They're like children. We'll scare them away. Boo!"

And the Romans believed them, did they?
What else could they do? Especially when their army was 200 miles away.

So when Boudicca's warriors burst in they were taken completely by surprise. They didn't stand a chance. Most were slaughtered straight away. However, a few citizens rushed into the temple and used it as a fort, even though it was unfinished.

So that was no good.

Well, they didn't do too badly. They resisted the onslaught for two whole days and nights and watched as tribesmen smashed down the statues, including the life-sized one of Claudius.

Yes, Boudicca was getting very fed up with all the stubborn people inside the temple. Something would have to be done to stop all this.

So what did she do?
Did she:

a) Say, "All right, you've done well. You deserve to go free"?

b) Say, "Come on out, surrender and we'll take you prisoner. Then, if you know what's good for you, you'll fight with us against the Romans"?

c) Say, "You ain't seen nothing yet"?

If you get this right, you'll know just what sort of person Boudicca was. Yes, it was **c)**.

a) This would have been a bit too sporting and they hadn't come for a bit of sport.

b) Why should she give her people extra mouths to feed when they'd have been useless warriors anyway and

36

trying to get back to the Romans all the time for a bit of comfort?

c) Now she could do something REALLY amusing. Amusing to the Iceni, that is.

The citizens watched as she directed her men to put piles of brushwood against the temple foundations and set fire to it. Then they watched as flames got higher and higher until they were all burnt out.

They heard Boudicca say: "Now pray to whatever gods you may have." They saw her point to her daughters and heard her cry: "And as you die, remember what you did to them." Then they heard and saw no more. The destruction of Camulodunum was complete.

And weren't the Iceni well pleased with that! Boudicca, a diadem and golden torque round her neck, could arouse yet more fighting spirit in her men. It had been a great victory.

Frumentum News

(update)

SURVEYORUM ANNUAM

Our Roman roadbuilders are making rapid progress in Roman Britain!

Roman soldiers supervise turf clearing by willing British prisoners, while our trained surveyors scan for fires on the horizon with a 'groma', a device to set out the line of the road.

We have a 200-year plan. By the end of stage 12, these roads will be in place. Ermine Street will run between Londinium and Eboracum. Watling Street will go from Portus Dubris to Viroconium. Stane Street will link Noviomagus to Londinium. There are even plans for a Neros Street that will run from Dunboniorum to Trimontium.

We plan walking, riding and charioting without any delays, jams, blocks or especially ambushes by dirty wild men with very few clothes on and nasty pointed spears.

So the Romans gave up and said, "All right, Boudicca. Have it your way," did they?

Did they heck as like. News of the rebellion reached Wales. Paulinus sent orders to the nearest legion, the 9th, in winter quarters at Longthorpe and Newton-on-Trent, to stop the rebels. Then, leaving his foot-soldiers to follow, Paulinus set out with his cavalry at full speed for Londinium.

This sounds like the end for Boudicca.

No, it wasn't. The 9th Legion had 2,000 foot-soldiers and 500 cavalry. Their commander was Petilius Cerealis. They marched quickly towards Camulodunum, thinking they'd *really* smash Boudicca and the babyish Britons.

But Boudicca and her warriors ambushed them along the road. They swept down from all sides, slashing, crashing and bashing everyone in front of them. The Romans had never before faced such bloodthirsty fierceness. Even their expert training couldn't save them. Only a wounded Petilius and 70 cavalry escaped.

So – it looked like Boudicca was unstoppable.

"VICTORY IS JUST A MATTER OF LUCK," said Boudicca, her wild eyes flashing. "ASK ANY FAILURE."

* * * *

CHAPTER 5

LONDINIUM'S
BURNING!

What next?

Well, nothing succeeds like success. More and more tribes joined Boudicca's warriors. Soon her horde was over 60,000 strong.

"Brilliant," said Boudicca.

Right, if you were Boudicca, what would you do now? Would you:

a) Say, "We've done all we need. They won't disturb us again. Let's go home"?

b) Say, "No letting up. Let's get on to Londinium and sort them out while they still don't know what's hit them"?

c) Have a party?

Surely she won't do **a)**. I don't suppose she'll do **c)**. It's got to be **b)**, hasn't it?
You're right, it wouldn't be **a)**. That would be *really* stupid. Anybody sane would think it would be **b)**, while the Romans were all over the place. Plenty of time for a party later, the longest in history.

But you'd be wrong. "Let's celebrate now," said her warriors. Yes, it was **c)**. For two weeks they ate, drank, danced and raided Roman farms. They sang songs about brave owls and mighty oaks and how Romans were wimps.

BUT WAS THIS WISE?

Probably not.
How right you are. Pity nobody thought so then. Paulinus did a lot during those two weeks. He continued his desperate dash from North Wales to Londinium.

When he arrived and heard of the 9th Legion's terrible fate he looked round him and knew he could not defend the town.

So he ordered the Romans to leave at once.

"And all other citizens as well," he said. "There's no way I can protect you."

He and his men retreated to the Midlands. There he waited for two more legions marching south-east along Watling Street.

Just a minute. If Boudicca had gone to Londinium straight away, she might have destroyed Paulinus as well.

43

She might indeed. Then things would have been a lot different. But when she finally reached Londinium, what did she find?

Londinium Evening Standard

GOVERNOR SAYS "STAY PUT!"

A Government statement issued today says the crowds heading towards Londinium are nothing to worry about.

"These people are thick as two short planks," officials say. "They cannot add II and II, or count up to to X, let alone do even the V times table. You don't want to let people like that get to you."

TODAY'S WEATHER

There will be no weather today. Metofficus, the weather forecasting soothsayer, is unfortunately under the weather today. Whether we will have weather tomorrow depends on whether Metofficus is still under the weather.

So, whatever the weather, HAVE A NICE DAY and KEEP OUT OF LONDINIUM. It may be very hot!

There were several thousand people who wouldn't leave Londinium. It was comfortable and profitable there. Why should they leave their wealth and good life? They clustered round where the Bank of England is now. Most were romanized British and believed something would stop Boudicca before she really did get to them.

Their stupidity stuck out like a carrot in a pancake. Boudicca's hordes were upon them before they knew it.

So that was the end of them, then?
It surely was. The British tribesmen had sworn to their gods that in revenge for how they'd been treated like slaves and their priests murdered, they would take no prisoners. Every single citizen was put to death and the officials were crucified. The warriors took everything of value and set fire to what was left. They then sat back to watch Londinium in flames.

"Burn, baby, burn... let this heat be felt right in the heart of Rome."

Screams of terror and chaos were replaced by sounds of crackling flames. Thick layers of burnt debris still lie beneath the City of London, marking out the red-hot passage of the British tribesmen.

And now they went home satisfied, did they?

So they swung north along Watling Street pursuing the retreating Paulinus. Soon there were 100,000 of them.

But perhaps it was too late already.

The Daily Thong

"ANOTHER VICTORY LIKE THIS AND WE'RE DONE FOR!"

Camulodunum completely crushed. Londinium lashed.

Britons merely cattle? Pull the udder one! When told that whenever Boudicca spoke she drew huge crowds, Paulinus said, "Yes, but when I rip her heart out the crowds will be even bigger. And you can quote me on that." So we have.

* * * *

CHAPTER 6

VERULAMIUM OR BUST

Why should the Trinovantes (another Celtic tribe) especially want to bust Verulamium?

I'm glad you asked that. Verulamium wasn't just a Roman town. It was also the ancient capital of another British tribe, the Catevellauni. Not only were they allies of the Romans but also, led by their king, Cymbeline, they had once conquered the Trinovantes, murdering many of them.

"Verulamium or bust, bust Verulamium," cried the Trinovantes. "It's coming home, it's coming home: revenge is coming home." Are you surprised? In their minds their disastrous defeat still burned bright. They wanted Verulamium to burn brighter still. And after victory at Camulodunum and Londinium, they were REALLY UP FOR IT.

So what sort of place was this Verulamium now?
The citizens loved it. They were especially proud of their big hole in the ground, which they called their amphitheatre. They loved shopping. They had an interesting range of shops, where they could buy anything from pots to more pots and a nice range of apples. They really enjoyed Verulamium's relaxed atmosphere. A tortoise in speed, it was almost asleep most of

the time. Not a lot happened, and what did happened very slowly. One official collected rocks because he admired their pace of life.

What did they make of Boudicca's army?
Not a lot. They didn't have time. They couldn't believe the speed of the engulfing fury. A wave of fire consumed them. The Trinovantes especially swept over the earth defences as though they weren't there. They hacked, cut and stabbed like madmen, killing everyone without batting an eyelid. Then the town and all the surrounding farmsteads were razed to the ground.

So, another victory?
Definitely.

	Played	Won	Drawn	Lost
Boudicca	3	3	0	0

Killings for: untold numbers.
Killings against: not very many.

Boudicca had an unbeaten record. She watched flames flickering in the twilight around burning shops and the broken amphitheatre. Her eyes sparkled darkly as she imagined the ancient gods dancing in celebration.

Yes, a Celtic twilight. But this twilight signalled a new Celtic dawn and an end to the Romans in Britain. She hoped.

"We'll forgive our enemies," she said. "But only when every last one of them is dead."

Her warriors hailed their great queen and her daughters marvelled at their magnificent mother.

Here she was, at a high moment of triumph. What would she do now? Would she:

a) Say, "Enough is enough. I've made my point. The Romans won't dare bother with us any more"?

b) Say, "This Verulamium could be a nice place if we built it up again. We could live here with the Trinovantes and have a great time"?

c) Say, "I want more than this"?

Well, there's no argument, is there? She's bound to choose c).

And she did.

Who would she be after next?
There was only one choice and she knew who it was.

PAULINUS.

"This is a step I must tread hard on if I am to rise higher," she said to herself and anyone else who would listen. "PAULINUS MUST DIE."

So she moved north-west along Watling Street. Her horde still grew as hundreds of carts filled with families joined them, agog to see every new triumph along the way. A farmstead here, a village there, nothing could stand against them.

Yes, total victory was a huge present which the Britons were seeing unwrapped a bit at a time. Only Boudicca could peel back the final piece of wrapping.

CHAPTER 7

PAULINUS GETS
VERY CROSS

**What did Paulinus think when he heard about the
destruction of Verulamium?**
He was *livid*. Camulodunum, then Londinium – burnt to the
ground. Now Verulamium. 70,000 Roman citizens killed. This
was not good.

In fact, it was very, very serious.

Ah yes, but what did he actually do?

There were three things to consider:

Did he:

a) Say to Boudicca, "All right, let's call it quits. You have your part of the country and we'll have ours"?

b) Give Britain up and get everyone out, back to Rome?

c) Resolve to DESTROY BOUDICCA?

Nothing on this earth would make him do **a)**. The Romans shared their Empire with NOBODY.

Paulinus wouldn't even *think* of **b)**. But someone else would.

These losses and Boudicca's growing strength were making the Emperor Nero back in Rome think very hard. Was little, rainy, cold Britain worth all this trouble? Why not withdraw his armies and all Roman citizens?

Just think. If he had, Roman rule would have only lasted seventeen years. Our language, with its Latin roots, might have been very different and none of our roads would have been straight!

Fire Fighter's Monthly

TODAY'S HOT NEWS ...BOU-HOOOOO!

The Emperor Nero is said to be seriously fed up with news of Boudicca's victories in Britain. He is so heated up about it that he is to turn to playing the fiddle to take his mind off things.

"The music seems to melt my troubles away," said the Emperor, who then revealed that it will be "All Romans out of Britain" if things don't change very soon.

"It's a game of two halves and right now I'm sick as a parrot," said Nero. "Now, pick a tune, go on, go on. I'll soon be really hot on the fiddle. 'Burn, baby, burn' is quite a crisp melody. Come on, sing along."

But Nero was just being daft, as usual.

Yes, Paulinus chose **c)**, at once.

"I must act quickly," he said to himself. "Pulling out of Britain now would be as sensible as an elephant hanging off a cliff with its trunk wrapped round a daisy."

What did he do about it?

Even as Boudicca and her warriors were burning the last bits of Verulamium, Paulinus brought together the 14th and 20th Legions and all their auxiliaries. This gave him an army of 12,000 well-trained, disciplined troops who wouldn't stand any nonsense.

He talked to his troops to let them understand how important it was to stop Boudicca. On that depended their own fates and the future of Roman Britain.

"I don't want us to achieve immortality through what we do here," he cried. "I want us to have it by not being killed by bloody Queen Bou and her horrible hordes."

How did he mean to stop her?

First, he sat down to think about his enemy. He'd heard a lot about her. Even those who hated her couldn't deny her gifts. She looked STUNNING. She was a natural leader. Her words stirred the blood of her warriors to incredible bravery.

But Paulinus said, "I'm not bad myself. I've just demolished all the druids in Britain. That took some doing. I invented my own flat-bottomed boats, invaded Anglesey on them and captured the place. Although I say it myself, that was brilliant.

Yes, I'll stand up to Boudicca, no matter what she throws at us."

Then he looked at the enemy's armies. Boudicca's huge following, well over 100,000 strong, was living off the fat of the land. Though they were on the move all the time they gathered new riches on the way. They feasted on new-laid eggs, chickens, goats, oysters, mussels and, of course, as much pork as they could shove down their throats. Oh yes, and the wine and beer flowed as they ate like birds – little tiny birds. That is, they swallowed seven times their own body weight each day.

Boudicca's hordes were happy. Happiness is like food: share it with others and you have a picnic!

They say an army marches on its stomach. Well, these stomachs were certainly full.

So we're coming up to the BIG ONE, are we?
We certainly are.

Let's look at the two sides and their leaders.

First, Boudicca. She and her Britons had timed their effort brilliantly. They bowled over everyone before them. They believed in THEMSELVES. They believed they were RIGHT. They were the way forward for AD 61 – the future for THE NEW BRITISH MILLENNIUM.

She and Paulinus were on a collision course. Perhaps Fate had decreed it would be like this from the day each was born.

What about Paulinus? In some ways, he and Boudicca were remarkably similar.

Both believed they were totally right.

Both had families they cared for deeply.

Both had great visions for what Britain should be.

Both were inventive and artistic.

And both were completely ruthless in warfare and knew there wasn't room for the two of them in 'their' new Britain.

A new age was dawning – but whose it was going to be was up for grabs.

But Boudicca was sure she was going to win, wasn't she? I wonder. She took a brief night's rest. Earth spirits were all around her. She turned her eyes to the moon, full of magic – *and suddenly she saw her dead husband, Prasutagus.*

"BEWARE, BOU," he said as he began to fade away again. "BEWARE THE BATTLE AHEAD."

CHAPTER 8

THE BATTLING BRITS
IN BITS

Just a minute. Didn't you say Boudicca had 100,000
warriors and Paulinus just 12,000?
I did.

Then it would be a carve-up, wouldn't it?
Not so. I also said the Roman troops were well trained and
disciplined.

Here's how Paulinus planned the battle. The site of the battle was in south Northamptonshire, near Watling Street in the Midlands – a valley narrow at one end, widening into a plain at the other. There were hills on each side and a thick forest at the narrow end. When Paulinus saw this, he knew at once what to do.

Yes, many legionaries were nervous. Some were afraid and a few might have run away if they could, for news of Boudicca and her warriors was terrifying. But Paulinus knew well that when they came to it they would fight and, even more important, that they would obey orders.

He drew his soldiers into a defensive position with the forest behind them. They were experienced and well-drilled. They had clear chains of command. They checked their armour, made sure everything was in the right place, their shields strong, short swords sharp and javelins at the ready.

Then the wind brought a strange sound, nerve-wracking, a sound like a fist in the stomach: the sound of 100,000 people out for their blood coming boldly towards them.

The smell in the air was electric. Fear, sweat, animal fat, Celtic herbs – above all the smell of approaching murder.

Then the wind changed.

THE TENSION WAS RISING.

Boudicca and her warriors swarmed on to the plain. She ordered the family wagons in a semi-circle round the rear of the valley, so they would have a grandstand view of the latest victory.

Then she drove up and down the British lines in her chariot, firing them up to fight.

"The gods will grant the revenge we deserve. Think of how many of us are fighting and why. We will win this battle or die.

That is what I, your Queen, plan to do. If we don't win, we'll be slaves. You can live as slaves if you want to. I won't. Have the courage to follow your hearts!"

The Britons listened and were moved. For a fleeting moment, Paulinus and Boudicca caught sight of one another and looked eye to eye. There was an understanding, a sneaking respect and a knowledge that: THIS ISLAND ISN'T BIG ENOUGH FOR THE BOTH OF US AND ONE OF US WILL DIE.

NOW THE COUNTDOWN WAS NEARLY OVER.

The Britons' wicker chariots carried warriors from one part of the battlefield to another. Once they reached their 'hot spots' the warriors would jump down to fight hand to hand on foot. This they prepared to do, bracing themselves for the battle to come.

Almost ready, they stared at the two Roman legions and laughed at the small selection of soldiers in front of them. 12,000 versus 100,000. Nearly ten to one. No contest. They were certain they'd win now.

For what seemed hours but was merely minutes the two sides stood still... then Boudicca's warriors sounded their war horns.

THE BATTLE WAS ON!

Round 1

The Britons made a mass charge, screaming mad for more triumph. On foot, they charged bravely. A line of Romans fell. Even so, try as they might, they were unable to break through the Roman ranks.

Round 2

Under Paulinus' orders, the Romans moved shrewdly and showered the British with javelins. The Romans wore armour. Boudicca's warriors fought half-naked. The javelins found their mark. Wave upon wave of Britons collapsed.

Round 3

The valley was serving the Romans well. Boudicca shouted directions to her Britons. Paulinus used his controlled chain of command. The Britons found themselves crowded together because of the hills each side of the valley and could not move easily. The Romans stood their ground.

You know, life's like a shower. One wrong turn and you're in really hot water. Now the Britons had nowhere left to turn. The showers of javelins continued. The Britons weakened.

Round 4

Now the Romans, in a strong wedge formation, advanced. They hacked with their short swords. Boudicca's warriors, with slings, spears and long clumsy swords were at a complete disadvantage as they tried to fight off this mass of Roman soldiers which sliced through them like a human tank.

Round 5

Now the Britons were in disarray as the Roman cavalry attacked. The Britons fell back. The Romans were unstoppable. They just

kept moving forward. The Britons started to retreat and tried to run away from the plain. With the Romans right behind them they frantically attempted to escape. But their way was barred by the semi-circle of wagons and chariots full of their families, still watching wide-eyed this terrible turn of events.

Round 6

Paulinus gave precise commands.

"No such rebellion shall take place again."

His soldiers closed in in tight terminator formation. They killed all who stood in their way: nearly 80,000 men, women and children. Boudicca's two daughters died. The Romans lost just under a thousand men.

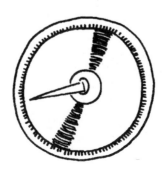

But Boudicca was swept away by thousands of escaping Britons, who believed that as long as she lived then all was not lost.

CHAPTER 9

BYE BYE BOU, WE'LL REMEMBER YOU

What was Boudicca thinking as she was spirited away by her surviving warriors?

Who can tell. After all, experience is what you have left when you've lost everything else. To say this was a bad experience for Boudicca is like saying frog spawn soup is not the first thing on your mind when you're hungry.

She had lost 80,000 of her people: men, women and children. Among them were her two daughters. Nothing seemed left but to die and become immortal. About as funny as swallowing a carthorse.

So is that what she did?
Not yet. She might be full of sorrow, but she felt there was still something further to do.

Whatever it was, would the Romans let her?
Not if they could help it. They were taking a horrible vengeance. Fugitives from the battle were hunted down relentlessly. As they ran, they threw away treasures they had looted when they destroyed Camulodunum, Londinium and Verulamium. From time to time, some of the loot still turns up

in East Anglia – a life-size head of Claudius found in the River Alde and a beautiful bronze helmet at Hawkedon in Suffolk.

Most of all, Paulinus wanted to capture Boudicca. He pushed on deeper into East Anglia, burning granaries and causing famine. He wasn't wasting time in letting everybody know just how angry the rebellion had made him.

Where had it all gone wrong for Boudicca?

She could so easily have won. But the Britons wasted time getting to Londinium while they were celebrating for two weeks after crushing Camulodunum. That let the Romans regroup. Besides, other Celtic tribes refused to join in the rebellion. Together, those two things made all the difference.

Where was she heading?

Her sacred oak grove, like a child winding back towards the womb that gave it birth. The time of Beltane beckoned. No druids left – but the ancient gods were a beacon to her.

Was Nero pleased about Paulinus' victory?

Yes – but he wasn't going to let it happen again either. More legions would come to Britain from Germany. That should stop any further rebellions.

Paulinus was pleased about this. But HE WANTED TO FIND BOUDICCA FIRST. While she was alive there was still a threat and he feared her still.

Will she get to the grove in time?
She wasn't there yet. For the Warrior Queen there was no rest. What peace is there between the hammer and the anvil? Perhaps her dreams were wrong all along.

On she went, deeper into the forests. Even in defeat she was a striking figure and more than once, when she could have been caught, her pursuers turned aside after all. There was still an inner strength radiating from her.

But Paulinus was determined to capture her. He would make an example of her – a lesson to all Britons who might think to rebel in future. He'd never known anyone like Boudicca and he needed to control her.

She was close to the heartland of her Iceni heritage, the place where she was once a baby, before it all began. But Paulinus was closing in. His troops drew up and spread round the sacred oak grove.

Now came the very last act in Boudicca's life.

"I have come for you," said Paulinus. "Give yourself up and I shall let you live."

Boudicca raised her spear, her eyes on fire.

"My life is not yours to give or take. I shall never be anyone's slave."

Paulinus stared at her. Like an unfinished dictionary that stops at 'nothing', words failed him.

The poison she took acted quickly. Her last words were, "I have my freedom. I am going home."

As she fell, her eyes closed. Prasutagus took her hand. Their two daughters were with them. They were one with the sparkling stars.

CHAPTER 10

THE NEXT 400 YEARS AND BEYOND

So that was it then. What happened next?

Boudicca's death in AD 61 was a major milestone in the course
of British history. For the next 400 YEARS Britain was
controlled by the *Pax Romana* – the Peace of Rome. That's as if
it had been started during the reign of Queen Elizabeth I and
had lasted right up until now. That's one-fifth of the last two
millennia. Mostly that's a VERY LONG TIME to stick to one set
of rules. But with Boudicca gone, it seemed that there was no-
one left to stand up to the bullying tactics of the Romans.

To All True Brits
NERO'S NEW YEAR'S NEWSLETTER
Roman Victory Special

OYSTERS AND WINE FOR THE 'VILLA' SET

No, no, no. Britain is not occupied by Romans. We are a mixture of Romans, Celtic tribes and people who have arrived much earlier. NO ASYLUM SEEKERS HERE. Boudicca tried it on and blew it.

We will not make this Province a desert and call it peace. Listen, we'll do everything right for you and all will be welcome to see our wonderful way of life that will last for 1000 years under Roman guidance. Transport's great. Just look at these fantastic straight roads.

Chariots available on easy terms (no spikes on wheels and no speeding). Everyone can be part of the villa set. Easy terms available and swallow hard.

Of course, if you don't want to go along with Roman rule, then on your own heads be it. (Off with your own heads, more like.)

FOOD NEWS
Yum yum, pig's bum:
Prime roast pig's bottom at bargain prices PLUS Chickens going cheep!

STOP PRESS!
Rumours from Gaul say that Rome is burning but Nero is STILL playing his fiddle!

After Boudicca, I reckon the Romans would have been horrible.
Well, for a while, Roman rule did become tougher. But then, in
AD 78, there was a new Governor of Britain. Agricola. He once
served in Paulinus' army. Agricola was humane and reasonable.
Most Britons became contented Roman subjects.

"Ah, it's not so bad really."

"True. Pass a piece of dormouse pie, please. Scrummy!"

Agricola had realized that Roman harshness made
Boudicca act the way she did. He wasn't going to make the
same mistake.

And did Britons stay that way?

They did. The spirit of rebellion died. Boudicca became a distant memory. The Romans introduced gracious living. They created towns throughout the island. The Britons weren't natural town-dwellers, but they got used to them, with their roads, bath houses, inns, shops and theatres. A soft, indulgent life – many tribes liked it a lot.

"How's the pigeon brain mousse?"

"Lovely, darling. Turn the heating up, I'm going to have a bath in sixteen sand grain's time."

Only many tribes? Not all?

Not those in the north, especially in Scotland. They believed in what Boudicca had said to her warriors 100 years before. "Romans are rude and unjust. They don't know right from wrong. Are they really men? Or are they something lower and weaker? They need warm water to wash in. They eat fancy food. They like soft cushions to lie their heads on when they sleep. Wimps or what?"

So Boudicca's words lived on in some men's hearts and the
Roman army was always busy somewhere in Britain.

But time waits for no-one and always moves on.

What's that supposed to mean?

 In time everyone forgot Boudicca.

 In time the Roman empire went. So everyone forgot Rome as well.

 In time the Dark Ages (Knight time?) rose up, then faded away again.

 In time the Anglo Saxons ruled, the Vikings invaded then the Normans conquered the lot. 1066 and all that.

 The film is on fast forward. History runs hysterically by, never stopping.

 Where's Boudicca in all this? Nowhere to be seen. A blur at best.

 1600 years went by. Then historians remembered her. She became more than just a name. What did she do? Why had she done it? People began to wonder.

 Now all the myths and legends got a kick start.

Myths and legends? Has all this been a load of lies, then?
No. Truth can be stranger than fiction but sometimes not as popular. Some people believed Boudicca was buried at Stonehenge. Others wanted to call her 'Boadicea' because it sounds more romantic.

"Yep, rolls off the tongue a treat."

The True Brit who fought the invader to keep her freedom. Great stuff. Along with the British Empire (in which True Brits made sure other people *didn't* have their freedom), she grew more and more popular. In 1902 it peaked when a great, heroic statue of 'Boadicea' was put up on London's Westminster Bridge. She's riding a chariot with blades sticking out of the wheels. Not good to get in the way of, but COMPLETELY WRONG.

She became the FIRST real woman leader of 'Britain' – a legend – the first person who somehow made the British empire greater than the Roman. A symbol of British pride: that's why more and more people believed in her.

That was years ago. Things have changed, haven't they?
Not really. Archaeologists, whose careers, after all, lie in ruins, dug up everything they could on her. So now her story can be told properly.

And children made up a famous verse about her, which went:

When Boudicca was on the road,
She didn't obey the Highway Code
And if she met a Roman crew
Cried, "Fancy running into you!"

Plates, coins and mugs with images of Boudicca on them were made for the Millennium.

There's even a British space satellite being discussed called *Boudicca One* (Romans nil). To infinity and further. Next stop the Universe.

So she was quite a lady!

Yes. Brave, fierce and ruthless, yet sometimes a dreamer with both feet planted firmly in the clouds, she somehow outlived all her enemies. No-one knows how Paulinus died or where he is buried. But Boudicca may one day be on her way to Alpha Centauri and onwards, carried ahead of myth, longer than legend – into realms of light beyond our knowledge.

In 2,000 years' time, perhaps another space probe called *Iceni* will follow her, as they always did, ahead of anything we now think possible. They'll meet Boudicca again, some time, somewhere.

Look up at the night sky, the sparkling stars. Can you somewhere see Boudicca?

Boudicca lives.

Long live Boudicca.

Boudicca and beyond...

THE END?

titles in the series